Once Upon a Dime

Dime

A Math Adventure

Nancy Kelly Allen

Illustrations by Adam Doyle

☗ Charlesbridge

For Larry, my husband — N.K.A.

For Linn — A.D.

Text copyright © 1999 by Nancy Allen Kelly
Illustrations copyright © 1999 by Adam Doyle

Published by Charlesbridge Publishing, 85 Main Street, Watertown, MA 02472
• (617) 926-0329 • http: / /www.charlesbridge.com

Printed in the United States of America
10 9 8 7 6 5 4 3 2

Library of Congress Cataloging-in-Publication Data
Allen, Nancy Kelly, 1949-
    Once upon a dime: a math adventure / by Nancy Kelly Allen; illustrated by Adam Doyle.
    p.   cm.
    Summary: Farmer Worth discovers that a special tree on his farm produces different
kinds of money, depending on what animal fertilizer he uses.
    ISBN 1-57091-161-4 (softcover)
    [1. Money — Fiction. 2. Farm Life — Fiction.]   I. Doyle, Adam, 1975- ill. II. Title.
PZ7.K2986On 1999
[E]—DC21   99-11928
                                              CIP

Once upon a time, way back in Birdhaven Hollow, there lived a farmer named Truman Worth. Every day, he worked from sunrise until sundown. He milked the cow, gathered the eggs, fed the pigs, and chased the sheep away from the briar patch. He was a friendly sort, so I liked to help him.

3

Even through the coldest winters, the wettest springs, the driest summers, and the windiest autumns, Farmer Worth whistled as he worked.

Some days, Miss Nancy True, who lived down the road, would drop by and hum along. With the cow mooing, the chickens clucking, the pigs oinking, and the sheep baaing, it sure was a symphony of noises.

Farmer Worth always said he was as happy as a pig in a puddle.

Farmer Worth grew crops just like everybody else in these parts. He grew apples, plain old regular apples. He grew beans, plain old regular beans. All the animals on the farm were just plain old regular animals, too.

As for fertilizer, Farmer Worth used only the organic kind. It was completely natural. After the animals provided it, and it dried out for about a year, it was as good as any chemical fertilizer you could buy; maybe better.

Only one plant on that farm was not plain or regular.
No one had planted it. It just sprouted up in a place
where nothing ever grew before.

When Farmer Worth saw that little wisp of a tree,
he scratched his head. "Now how did that happen?" he
asked his cow, Moolly Pitcher. The cow rolled her great
brown eyes.

Farmer Worth thought any tree that grew in that
spot would surely need some fertilizer. He fetched a
bucket of old chicken droppings and dumped it
around the little tree.

In just one week, the tree was as high as my knees. In two weeks, it was up to my shoulders. In three weeks, it was as tall as Farmer Worth.

Soon, little buds appeared, and we watched as the buds opened into flowers. In the center of each flower was a penny. That tree grew the most beautiful crop of pennies you ever did see. They glinted copper in the sunshine.

"Well, now," said Farmer Worth. He plucked a penny and polished it on his shirt. "A penny for your thoughts," he told me.

"We're rich! We should count it all up!" I crowed as loud as his rooster, Franklin D. Roostervelt.

Farmer Worth grinned. "Be my guest," he said. He held out a handful of corn for his chickens, Lewis and Cluck.

By the time I finished picking, there were 100 pennies. Farmer Worth put the pennies in an old pickling jar. Then he gathered up some nails and fixed up the henhouse. He had the happiest chickens you ever did see.

That fall, we shoveled an old pile of pig squish all around the bottom of that penny tree.

The following spring, little silver centers grew in flowers all over the tree. "I declare," sang Miss True when she brought us a plate of homemade brownies, "Your tree is sprouting nickels, Mr. Worth!"

"I call it my piggy bank tree," said Farmer Worth, scratching his pig behind the ears. Dwight D. Oikenhower grunted happily.

I got a pail and picked 100 nickels. Farmer Worth added up the nickels and put them in the jar with the pennies. To celebrate, he turned on the hose for Dwight D. Oikenhower, William Muckinley, and Dolly Madisow. Those pigs made the ooziest mudhole you ever did see.

That fall, Farmer Worth decided to try sheep biscuits as fertilizer for the tree.

The next spring, when buds appeared on the tree, I watched them like a cat at a mouse hole. They were very small when they started to open. "These ain't big enough for nickels, Farmer Worth!" I said.

"*Aren't* big enough," corrected Miss True, who used to be a teacher.

"But they're worth twice as much," said Farmer Worth, looking closely. "These flowers are making dimes!"

"And don't they make a lovely sound," said Miss True. She closed her eyes to listen. The dimes pinged and tinged, clinked and plinked, making the tree sound like wind chimes. Folks said you could hear the music all through the hollow.

Farmer Worth liked the music so much, he didn't pick any of the dimes. After a week or so, they started falling to the ground. I raked them up and counted them. All in all, I poured 100 dimes into the jar like a silver waterfall.

To celebrate, Farmer Worth mixed up a tub of sheep dip for Wooldrow Wilson, Grover Clevelamb, Rutherford Baa Hayes, and all the other sheep. It was the bubbliest sheep dipping you ever did see.

That fall, we talked about the strange tree a lot. It had grown bigger and would need more fertilizer. Farmer Worth decided to use cow pies.

Farmer Worth and I raked in old cow pies as far as the branches of the tree reached.

Next spring, the flower buds grew bigger and bigger.

When the buds opened, each flower had a shiny new quarter growing in the middle.

The heavy quarters made a sound like tiny cowbells. They didn't sound as nice as those dimes, but they sure were worth a lot more. When we were done picking, we had 100 quarters to add to the jar.

"I reckon we have a cup of quarters. That's a quarter of a quart of quarters," joked Farmer Worth. I tried to say it three times fast.

Farmer Worth patted Moolly Pitcher and said, "Look what we grew!" He then gave Moolly a shiny new cowbell.

Now we had used fertilizer from each kind of animal on the farm. Farmer Worth was going to fertilize the tree with the same old cow pies, when I had an idea. "How about my Dad's bull?" I asked. "Dad would let us use some bull chips."

"He might," said Farmer Worth. "But will the bull?"

Well, I thought that bull was pretty friendly, so I paid him a visit. He didn't like me much, but I came home with a whole sack of bull chips for the tree.

The next spring,
the tree didn't flower at all. It just
made leaves. From the barn, it
looked like every other tree on
the farm. I was as sad as a
turkey who's lost its gobble.

One day, Farmer Worth
remarked that the tree looked a
little odd. He went over to it for
a closer look. Suddenly, he gave
a whoop so loud that Miss True
and I came running.

19

Turned out, those green leaves had George Washington's picture on them. They were one-dollar bills!

The dollars rustled in the breeze. Farmer Worth, Miss True, and I had a picnic and a picking party. One hundred crisp dollar bills nested in our basket.

That summer, when Farmer Worth visited the zoo, he came home laughing and showed me a sack of Chinese panda patties that he brought back with him. That fall, we worked them into the soil around the tree.

In the spring, new green leaves grew all over the tree. Would they be dollar bills or five-dollar bills — maybe even ten-dollar bills? I went over to check the tree every day.

Then, something very peculiar happened. The green leaves changed to a beautiful red and white. "Look at this, Farmer Worth," I said. "It's not real money."

"Oh, it's real money all right," explained Farmer Worth. "These are real, honest-to-goodness yuan, Chinese dollars. And we've got a bumper crop."

By now, Farmer Worth had saved up quite a bit of money. He and Miss True got married, filled their pockets with yuan, and set sail on a slow boat to China for their honeymoon.

Farmer Worth left the running of the farm to me. This was my big chance. I had always wondered what would happen if two different kinds of fertilizers were mixed together. Would two kinds of money grow, and if they did, how much?

What about pig squish and chicken droppings? After all, ham and eggs go well together. If the tree grew 100 pennies when it was fertilized with chicken droppings, and 100 nickels when it was fertilized with pig squish, then what would it grow with both?

The next spring, I was hoping for hundreds of pennies and nickels, but the tree grew only 50 of each. I figured out how much money that added up to, and put the coins in the jar, but I was really disappointed.

The next fall, Franklin D. Roostervelt marched around the cow as if he were trying to tell me something, so I fertilized the tree with chicken droppings and cow pies.

In the spring, the tree grew
75 quarters and 75 pennies.
I was happy as a chicken
in a wagon full of corn,
until I added it all up.
It was not as much
as I thought.

The next fall, I decided to use cow pies, because there were so many of them. What would be the best thing to mix them with?

That day, as I walked past the bull, I had an idea.

"Of course!" I shouted. "What that tree needs are cow pies and bull chips! Cows and bulls are the biggest animals around, after all."

Next spring, the tree grew
100 quarters and 100 dollar
bills. I couldn't wait to show
Farmer Worth.

That very day, Farmer Worth returned from China. We all rushed out to meet him. The chickens clucked a melody, and the pigs oinked in harmony. The sheep bleated a greeting, and the cow mooed halloo. It was the most joyful homecoming you ever did see.

I told Farmer Worth all about my fertilizer mixing experiments. "I reckon we should use even bigger animals now," I finished. "Elephant mounds might be the very thing."

Farmer Worth thanked me and told me what a great job I'd done on the farm. That evening, Miss Nancy True — I mean, Mrs. Nancy Worth — remarked how much I'd grown while they were gone. Together, they told me all about their trip and showed me pictures of China.

That night, they decided that they wanted to go back to fertilizing the tree with sheep biscuits. "The money's not all that important," they said, "And nothing we saw or heard in our travels could equal the music of the dimes."

The next year when spring came, the sweet music of the dime tree could be heard whenever a breeze blew. The dimes pinged and tinged, clinked and plinked. Folks said you could hear the music all through the hollow.

I had to admit that I had missed the sound, too.

After that, nothing strange happened in Birdhaven Hollow
for a long, long time.

That is, until the day when we all found out that little
Annie True-Worth liked eating her alphabet cereal outdoors.